S0-AHM-496

BEHIND THE NEWS
VIOLENCE AGAINST WOMEN

Emma Marriott

CRABTREE
Publishing Company
www.crabtreebooks.com

DiPietro Library
Franklin Pierce University
Rindge, NH 3461

Crabtree Publishing Company
www.crabtreebooks.com
1-800-387-7650

Published in Canada
616 Welland Ave.
St. Catharines, ON
L2M 5V6

Published in the United States
PMB 59051, 350 Fifth Ave.
59th Floor,
New York, NY

Published in 2017 by CRABTREE PUBLISHING COMPANY.

All rights reserved. No part of this publication may be reproduced, stored in a retrieval system or be transmitted in any form or by any means, electronic, mechanical, photocopying, recording, or otherwise, without the prior written permission of the copyright owner.

First published in 2014 by Wayland
(A division of Hachette Children's Books)
Copyright © Wayland 2014

Author: Emma Marriott

Contributing writer and indexer: Janine Deschenes

Editorial director: Kathy Middleton

Editors: Jon Richards, Ellen Rodger, and Janine Deschenes

Designer: Malcolm Parchment

Proofreader: Wendy Scavuzzo

**Production coordinator
and prepress technician:** Ken Wright

Print coordinator: Katherine Berti

Photographs and reproductions:
Getty Images: © Chip Somodevilla: p 11; © Bill Nation/Sygma/Corbis p 14; © Stephen Barnes/Demotix/Corbis p 19; © JEWEL SAMAD: p 30; © Annibale Greco/Corbis p 33; © Eduardo Munoz Alvarez: p 37; © MONEY SHARMA/epa/Corbis p 40; © Kevin Winter: p 42; © Spencer Platt: p43;

Keystone: © Imago: p 23; © Tom Williams: p 28

Shutterstock: Tatiana Belova: front cover (bottom right); © arindambanerjee: title page (top left); © JStone: pp 3 (top right), 22; © Paul Lurrie: front cover (top), p 5; © arindambanerjee: front cover (bottom left), p 17; © Helga Esteb: p 21; © a katz: p 36; © Saikat Paul: p 44; © Asianet-Pakistan: p 45;

Wikimedia: title page (bottom), pp 41, 3 (bottom left), 6, 7, 10, 15, 16, 18, 20, 24, 26, 27, 31, 35, 41

All other images by Shutterstock

Cover: Nearly 300 women took part in a One Billion Rising flash mob dance to protest violence against women in Washington Square Park in New York City (top); Women playing music during the 9th Annual Strawberry Ceremony in Toronto, ON, to remember the missing and murdered indigenous women (bottom left); Domestic violence victim (bottom right)

Printed in Canada/072016/PB20160525

Library and Archives Canada Cataloguing in Publication

Marriott, Emma, author
     Violence against women / Emma Marriott.

(Behind the news)
Includes index.
Issued in print and electronic formats.
ISBN 978-0-7787-2590-9 (hardback).--
ISBN 978-0-7787-2595-4 (paperback).--
ISBN 978-1-4271-1772-4 (html)

     1. Women--Crimes against--Juvenile literature. 2. Abused women--Juvenile literature. 3. Violent crimes--Juvenile literature. I. Title.

HV6250.4.W65M3337 2016   j362.88082   C2016-902560-8
                                                                          C2016-902561-6

Library of Congress Cataloging-in-Publication Data

Names: Marriott, Emma, author.
Title: Violence against women / Emma Marriott.
Description: New York : Crabtree Publishing, 2016. | Series: Behind the news | Includes index.
Identifiers: LCCN 2016016656 (print) | LCCN 2016018472 (ebook) | ISBN 9780778725909 (reinforced library binding) | ISBN 9780778725954 (pbk.) | ISBN 9781427117724 (electronic HTML)
Subjects: LCSH: Women--Crimes against--Juvenile literature. | Abused women--Juvenile literature. | CYAC: Women--Crimes against--Juvenile literature. | Violent crimes--Juvenile literature.
Classification: LCC HV6250.4.W65 M3337 2016 (print) | LCC HV6250.4.W65 (ebook) | DDC 362.88082--dc23
LC record available at https://lccn.loc.gov/2016016656

CONTENTS

A violation of human rights....4
The longer view......................6
Who and why? 8
Grooming of young girls.........10
How common is grooming?....12
Behind closed doors...............14
Missing women in Mexico......16
What is human trafficking?...18
Extreme oppression 20
Shooting of a school girl........22
Should others interfere? 24
Gender violence.....................26
How does the media act? 28

Weapons of war....................30
Mass rape of Congolese
women...................................32
The effects of rape................34
Challenging violence..............36
Gang rape in Delhi.................38
Who was to blame?................40
Combating rape culture...........42
Taking action to end
violence...............................44
Glossary 46
Index....................................48

A VIOLATION OF HUMAN RIGHTS

Every week, the news brings us stories of violence against women and girls. From domestic abuse and **rape** to forced **abortions**, **female genital mutilation** (FGM), and murder, all are shocking examples of how violence affects women everyday and devastates lives around the world.

What is violence against women?

Violence against women can include physical, sexual, and **psychological** violence. It can involve overt, or visible, acts of violence, such as murder and rape, as well as more hidden forms of abuse, such as forced marriage and the trafficking of women into **prostitution** or slavery.

The most common form of violence happens within a marriage or partnership. This is called **domestic violence**, or intimate partner violence. Violence against women, including intimate partner violence or domestic violence, happens in all communities, in the home, at school, and work. Abusers come from all walks of life.

Many organizations across the world are working to combat violence against women. The United Nations (UN) has pledged, under its UNITE campaign launched in 2008, to raise public awareness and political support to prevent all forms of violence against women and girls.

Intimate partner violence can happen in the home or anywhere, at the hands of people women know and love, including partners of all genders.

So many questions

We might question the reasons why violence still happens to so many women across the world. Who might experience violence, and what are some of the personal and global effects of violence against women? How can we stop it from happening? We often turn to television, newspapers, and computers for our information. But, we need to ask questions about the media, too. How does the media portray violence against women? In this book, we go behind the news to address these difficult questions.

These women are taking part in a flash mob dance in Washington Square Park, New York City. It was organized by "One Billion Rising," a group that campaigns around the world against the rise in violence against women.

"At least one in every three women globally has been beaten, coerced into sex, or otherwise abused in her lifetime, with rates reaching 70 percent in some countries."

United Nations Development Fund for Women

THE LONGER VIEW

Violence against women has a long history that reflects **patriarchal** beliefs that view men as rightfully more powerful and deserving than women. The extent of violence has always been difficult to measure because, even today, the vast majority of abuse is not reported by the victims.

Conflict and violence

Violence against women has been seen historically as an inevitable part of war. For example, armies of the ancient Greek, Persian, and Roman Empires were known to rape women in enemy communities.

• **During World War II (1939 to 1945), many women who lived in war-occupied countries were raped or abducted. An example is the "comfort girls" abducted by the Japanese army and forced into sexual slavery.**

• **In the Bosnian War (1992–1995), rape was used as a means of** ethnic cleansing **predominantly by Serbian soldiers targeting Bosnian women and girls.**

• **In 1994, in the eastern African state of Rwanda, rape was similarly used as a means of** genocide**, with women being intentionally impregnated by HIV-infected men.**

A global summit–End Sexual Violence in Conflict–was held in London in June 2014, co-chaired by former British Foreign Secretary William Hague along with UN Special Envoy actress Angelina Jolie.

This Russian poster urges the audience to "open your eyes" to violence against women and girls.

• **In response to this, international communities began to recognize rape as a weapon of war. In 2008, the UN Security Council affirmed that "rape and other forms of sexual violence can constitute** war crimes **[and] crimes against humanity..."**

Domestic violence

Within marriage, the law has been slow to **criminalize** sexual assault. Historically, women were considered the property of their husbands, so a man raping his wife was not considered a crime in most countries until the 1980s and 1990s. In the early 1800s, courts in most countries still viewed wife-beating as a husband's right. The laws and public attitudes towards intimate partner violence have changed in many countries around the world. But it is still difficult for women who have experienced violence to escape it or receive justice in court if a charge is laid.

• **Since the 1970s, changes sparked by feminist movements have called for law enforcement to treat intimate partner violence or sexual violence the same as other criminal assaults. This has brought issues of violence against women more into the public eye.**

• **While intimate partner violence is outlawed in the** Western world**, it is viewed differently in other countries where husbands and wives are not considered equals. Globally, nearly half of 15- to 19-year-olds think a husband is justified in beating his wife under certain circumstances.**

WHO AND WHY?

Who are the **perpetrators** of violence against women? Are some women more likely to experience abuse than others? Who is at greatest risk? Why does violence against women happen, and what are the factors that cause it?

Women of all ages

Violence, whether it is in the home, at school, or in a larger community, affects women and girls around the world. Violence is caused by a host of factors, from cultural and religious beliefs to **economic** pressures, previous exposure to violence, and warfare.

The victims

While violence affects an average of 35 percent of women globally, women are more likely to experience physical or sexual violence in certain regions of the world. In 2005, The World Health Organization (WHO) conducted a report on global domestic violence against

Many women who experience violence feel isolated and alone because they believe that the law and those around them will not protect them from further violence.

Easy access to alcohol and high levels of drinking can increase the risk of violence against women.

disability, age, or religion. A 2008 United Nations (UN) fact sheet showed that in Europe, North America, and Australia more than half of women who have disabilities experienced physical abuse, compared to one third of women without disabilities. In India, women from a lower caste, or social class, are more likely to experience high rates of sexual violence committed by men of a higher caste.

women. It found high numbers of women who were physically or sexually assaulted. The report noted that, while 15 percent of women in Japan had experienced violence by an intimate partner, a shocking 71 percent of women in Ethiopia had experienced violence. In addition to location, other factors that increase the likelihood of a woman experiencing violence is her **ethnicity**, class, **caste**,

The perpetrators

The perpetrators of violence are often known to their victims, such as in cases of intimate partner violence. But the Internet can allow perpetrators to abuse their victims anonymously. Often, victims choose not to report incidents of abuse. This is because they might experience shame from their families or communities, or are not protected or supported by national or state laws. This means that abusers are rarely held accountable.

WHO IS AT RISK?

In October 2013, the World Health Organization identified risk factors associated with intimate partner and sexual violence. It found that:

"Risk factors for being a perpetrator include low education, exposure to child maltreatment (abuse) or witnessing violence in the family, harmful use of alcohol, attitudes accepting of violence and gender inequality.

Risk factors for being a victim of intimate partner and sexual violence include low education, witnessing violence between parents, exposure to abuse during childhood, and attitudes accepting of violence and gender inequality."

GROOMING OF YOUNG GIRLS

On April 24, 2009, two teenagers stumbled out of a home in Derby, United Kingdom (U.K.), claiming they had been raped. Police had previously set up a surveillance operation after stopping a car with two teenagers who had been earlier reported missing. They would soon find out that the men in the car were the accused rapists and they were part of a gang that was sexually exploiting dozens of underaged girls.

NEWS FLASH

Date: 2009
Location: Derby, U.K.
Perpetrators: 13 men arrested, aged between 26 and 38 (11 stood trial)
Victims: 27 known teenage girls aged between 12 and 18
Type of violence: Grooming and sexual abuse of teenage girls

A gang of sexual predators cruised the streets of Derby in cars to groom and exploit teenage girls.

Wide-scale sexual abuse

The victims gave statements that led to the unearthing of a wide-scale sexual abuse ring, run by criminal gangs involving 27 teenage girls, the youngest of whom was 12. The men would meet the girls on the street, and invite them to drink, smoke, or take drugs. After, they would take them to a park, a secluded area, or a house, and rape them.

The rapes were often violent, sometimes involving five or six men who

> ## "I was personally shocked at the scale of the abuse we uncovered. It hadn't been reported and it was happening under the radar."
>
> **Detective Superintendent Debbie Platt, who led the police investigation**

would film the attacks on their phones. The girls would be threatened and some were held as prisoners.

Thirteen men were arrested and nine, including ring leaders Mohammed Liaqat, and Abid Saddique, were convicted of several offences that carried sentences from 18 months to seven and a half years.

Judge Philip Head told Saddique that he had embarked on a "reign of terror on girls in Derby."

After Dru Sjodin was kidnapped and murdered by a sexual offender who had been recently released from prison, the United States government enacted "Dru's Law," creating a National Sex Offender Public Registry, which lists sex offenders and allows the public to know if they live nearby.

VULNERABLE GIRLS

The girls in Derby were groomed by their attackers, which means they befriended them and gained their trust. One 16-year-old victim said: "they'd take you out, buy you ice creams, take you out for a lovely meal." Actions like these are meant to make the girls feel comfortable with their abusers. They also targeted girls who lived in group homes or who did not have family who could protect them. "They actually take advantage of the fact that no one does care about you really."

HOW COMMON IS GROOMING?

The targeting of young girls in Derby brought to light questions about sexual assault and grooming. Many wondered what led to the grooming in Derby, and how prevalent sexual grooming was in society.

Vulnerable girls

In Derby, the attackers went for young, vulnerable girls. Grooming is a common method of gaining trust used by sexual predators on children. They give their intended victim attention, compliment them, buy them things, and generally appear sympathetic to them in order to make them, and sometimes their families, feel at ease, or special. The idea is to manipulate the intended victim into being cooperative and reduce the chances that they will speak out about abuse.

The sexual exploitation of anyone

GROOMING

Often the victims of sexual grooming do not see themselves as victims. They sometimes believe they are in relationships with their abusers. This is because abusers manipulate victims using peer pressure, emotional blackmail, and substance abuse.

Peer pressure can be a powerful influencer among teens. Pressure within peer groups can lead to abuse from apparent "friends."

12

under 18 is a form of child abuse. Although boys and young men can be victims, girls and young women are most vulnerable. Often, sexual predators will claim that their "relationships" are consensual, meaning that the victim agreed to the abuse. But nobody can agree to abuse. The predator always holds the power in the relationship. With teenagers, predators often groom by getting their victims to exchange sex for some "reward" such as meals, a place to stay, money, or gifts. But that's not fair trade.

All children and young people can be at risk of sexual exploitation. But many victims of sexual predators are more vulnerable because of their history. Statistics show children and young people who have previously experienced maltreatment, or abuse, live in foster care, are involved with gangs, or have a history of running away, are more likely to be preyed upon by sexual predators.

EXPLOITATION

As access to the Internet increases, so does the exploitation of children online. The time between the initial contact between abuser and victim, and its outcome can be much shorter online, because an online environment allows abusers to deceive victims without location restraints. Cases include children being forced to perform sexual acts on webcam by sex abusers, who often pretend to be a child online then threaten to show their pictures publicly.

In September 2013, the U.K.'s Child Exploitation and Online Protection (CEOP) Command reported that in the previous two years 424 children in the U.K. had been victims of online sexual blackmail.

Internet exploiters hide their identities, hoping to fool young people into believing they are friends of the same age.

BEHIND CLOSED DOORS

Intimate partner violence is the most common form of violence against women. It includes physical, emotional, and sexual violence, as well as controlling behaviors on a woman by her partner. Much of it is hidden, and women who live with this violence live in fear.

Why is this violence hidden?

Various factors, including shame and fear of retaliation, contribute to women's reluctance to report intimate partner violence. Legal and criminal systems in many countries can make the process difficult. Some families and societies view violence within the home as normal behavior, and women end up learning to accept it. Poverty and economic dependence on a partner can make it difficult for women to remove themselves from a violent relationship. Each year in the United States, almost two million women are assaulted by an intimate partner. And those are just the reported assaults. In Canada, intimate partner violence accounts for up to one quarter of all police-reported violent crimes.

Former American football player and actor O.J. Simpson stood trial for the murder of his wife, Nicole Brown, in 1995. According to Brown's diaries, she had suffered from violence at his hands since 1985. Simpson was found not guilty.

These U.S. Immigration and Customs Enforcement (ICE) officers are arresting men they suspect of human trafficking in Houston, Texas, in February 2010.

Trafficking

Even extreme violence, in the form of murder and the disappearance of women, can go unnoticed. Trafficking for the purposes of forced labor or sexual slavery is hidden, and once women are forced into the world of prostitution, it is difficult for them to get out. Often, women imprisoned by human traffickers are dependent on their captors, who take any money they earn for themselves. In some cases, law enforcement does not see these women as victims, but as participants in illegal labor or sex industries.

Female **migrant** workers can also be subject to abuse by their employers, forced into hidden slavery. Often, they are unable to seek help because they are not considered citizens of the countries they had migrated to.

"Violence against women is a hidden epidemic, and hidden is a very important word. We all know that women are getting raped as a weapon of war in places like the DRC [Democratic Republic of the Congo], but in the developed world the problem is hidden."

Ann Veneman, the former Executive Director of UNICEF

MISSING WOMEN IN MEXICO

All around Ciudad Juárez, a city on the border with the United States, photographs of missing women are posted on lampposts, walls, and storefronts. Since 1993, hundreds of women have disappeared from the region, many of them raped, tortured, and murdered, and left in the desert that surrounds the city.

NEWS FLASH

Date: Since 1993
Location: Ciudad Juárez, Mexico
Perpetrators: Vast majority unknown
Victims: According to Amnesty International, more than 370 murdered, and many more have disappeared
Types of violence: Murder, sexual violence, and trafficking

These crosses were erected in Lomas del Poleo Planta Alta, Ciudad Juárez, where the bodies of eight of the women were found in 1996.

Ciudad Juárez

Various factors have been attributed to the murders of women in Ciudad Juárez. The city is a known location for drug trafficking, with wars between gangs and drug cartels fueling crime. The city also houses numerous factories, many of whose workers are women who have traveled from poor rural areas, and who are vulnerable to exploitation because they must work to survive. The growth in the factories in the last 20 years has also coincided with a growth in violence against women.

The Cuidad Juárez case isn't unique. In Toronto, the Strawberry Ceremony (right) draws attention to the more than 1,000 missing and murdered First Nations, Métis, and Inuit women in Canada since 1980. **Indigenous** women are seven times more likely to be murdered than non-Indigenous women in Canada. Recently, after much criticism, the government acted to investigate the reasons why by launching a National Inquiry into Missing and Murdered Indigenous Women.

Systemic misogyny, or the cultural attitude that entrenches prejudices against women and allows for the oppression of women and girls, is particularly pronounced in the factories, where female workers suffer abuse. Unsurprisingly, Ciudad Juárez has the highest levels of domestic violence in the country.

The local authorities and police have done little to investigate the women's disappearances or to convict perpetrators. The families of the missing and murdered women, and human rights organizations criticized the Mexican authorities, and accused state investigations of being mishandled. Mexico reformed its legal system in 2008, and since that time, although the murders have not stopped, more murderers have been prosecuted, found guilty, and sentenced to jail.

"The authorities have not the slightest interest in finding our daughters. Everybody's scared to speak up."

Olga Esparza, mother of an 18-year-old student who disappeared in 2009 after failing to return home from a university class

WHAT IS HUMAN TRAFFICKING?

What is human trafficking? Why do authorities often fail to see or stop these extreme cases of violence which, according to the United Nations Global Report on Trafficking in Persons, predominantly involves the sexual exploitation of women and girls. And why aren't more perpetrators convicted?

HUMAN TRAFFICKING

The United Nations (UN) states that human trafficking affects every country in the world, with the highest numbers of trafficking activity being sexual exploitation, followed by forced labor. Although the International Labor Organization (ILO) estimates that 2.4 million people worldwide are victims of trafficking, some studies show that the number could be as high as 30 million. Despite these high numbers, the UN found that less than 1 percent of perpetrators are convicted.

Against their will

Human trafficking is the illegal movement of people, most commonly for the purposes of forced labor and sexual slavery. People are held against their will and forced to provide services for their trafficker or for others. It is difficult to know how many people are trafficked worldwide, but a UN study estimated that, in 2014, 70 percent of victims were women or girls, and 33 percent were children.

While victims of human trafficking can come from any ethnic or social

Child slave workers are common in India. In spite of a government ban, some children are still sold by their parents when the family is extremely poor and cannot afford to feed and keep them.

background, they often tend to be in a vulnerable situation, far away from home, and in poverty. Many girls and women are trafficked in their home countries, and runaways and homeless youth are most at risk. In some countries, women and girls who are trafficked and forced to work as prostitutes cannot contact police. If they do, they are often arrested and sent back to the people who forced them into sex slavery.

Domestic workers, such as maids and nannies, are also vulnerable to trafficking. They may be citizens of the country they work in, foreign nationals with work visas, or undocumented immigrants. Domestic work situations become trafficking when an employer uses fraud, coercion, or force to control the worker. Some domestic workers are beaten or sexually assaulted, and told that they will be kicked out of the country, or their families will be harmed, if they speak out.

Soroptimist International, a global movement working to improve the lives of women, held a protest rally against human trafficking in Belfast, Northern Ireland, in October 2012. The first Soroptimist (a latin word meaning "best for women") club was founded in 1921 in Oakland, California.

"**Eventually I arrived in a bar in Kosovo, [and was] locked inside and forced into prostitution... In the bar I was never paid. I could not go out by myself, and the owner became more and more violent as the weeks went by. He was beating me and raping me and the other girls.**"

21-year-old woman from the country of Moldova, trafficked in Kosovo

EXTREME OPPRESSION

Violence against women occurs in every culture around the world. The beliefs and practices in some cultures mean that women are denied certain rights. In more than 50 countries around the world, for example, sexual assault within a marriage is not considered a crime. This reflects long-held beliefs that a woman is her husband's property.

> "Three million of the world's women are subjected to FGM every year with 10 percent dying as a result."
>
> *The Independent* **newspaper website**

This road sign near Kapchorwa, Uganda, is part of a worldwide campaign to raise awareness of the harm that results from FGM.

Genital mutilation

Female genital mutilation (FGM) is the removal of all or part of the external female genitalia. Around 140 million girls and women worldwide are living with the **consequences** of FGM. It is most common in Africa and some parts of Asia and the Middle East.

FGM is mostly carried out on young girls between infancy and 15 years of age, and is considered in some cultures to be a necessary part of raising a girl properly. Despite these beliefs, there are no medical benefits to the procedure. In fact, it commonly leads to infection, sterility, or the inability to have children, as well as complications with childbirth, newborn deaths, psychological problems, and even death.

Sharmeen Obaid-Chinoy is an Oscar-winning filmmaker and activist who uses her work to draw attention to honor violence in her home country of Pakistan. Her films Saving Face *and* Girl in the River: The Price of Forgiveness *detail the stories of survivors of honor violence.*

Honor violence

In some cultures, women represent the "honor" of a family. They are expected to dress and act modestly, not talk to boys or date, and marry a husband chosen, or arranged, by their family.

If a girl or woman falls in love with a boy or man not approved by her family, or if it is believed that through her behavior she has brought shame upon her family, she may experience emotional or physical abuse. She may even be murdered by her own family members in an "honor killing." Disputes over **dowries**, refusal to marry, requests to divorce, and other ways of going against a family's beliefs, such as dressing in a different way, or speaking publicly against her abuse, can also lead to violence. Although honor-based violence is mostly associated with South Asian and Middle Eastern countries, it happens around the world.

"I have met some of the victims. They speak about wedlock being used as a weapon and the horrors to which this can lead, such as rape, abuse, and unwanted pregnancy."

Sayeeda Warsi, British lawyer and former politician, 2011

SHOOTING OF A SCHOOL GIRL

On the afternoon of October 9, 2012, a **Taliban** gunman boarded a bus taking children home from school in Mingora, Pakistan. One of the schoolgirls was 14-year-old Malala Yousafzai. The gunman deliberately shot the defenseless girl in the head and neck, along with two of her classmates. All three girls survived the attack.

NEWS FLASH

Date: October 9, 2012
Location: Mingora in Swat Valley, northwest Pakistan
Perpetrators: The Taliban
Victim: 14-year-old Malala Yousafzai
Type of violence: Attempted murder by shooting

Malala Yousafzai was flown to the U.K. for surgery after the shooting, and spent many months recovering.

Speaking openly

Born in Pakistan's Swat Valley, since the age of 11 Malala had been anonymously writing a blog for the BBC about life as a girl under the **oppressive** rule of the Taliban. She spoke openly about the need for girls' education, something that the Taliban strongly opposes. The school bus shooting that targeted Malala horrified people across many political and religious groups. People voiced their disgust in the newspapers, on television, and through social media, leading to protests in many Pakistani cities.

After her attack, Malala Yousafzai spoke on the need for girls' education in front of the United Nations on her 16th birthday.

Malala survived the attack and now lives and goes to school in Birmingham, U.K. She regularly speaks about her firm belief in education for all children, has written a memoir, and won the Nobel Peace Prize in 2014. A UN petition launched under her name, "I am Malala," has led to the ratification, or official confirmation, of Pakistan's first Right to Free and Compulsory Education Bill. She has become an important voice, not only for girls' education, but for global female rights.

THE TALIBAN

The Taliban took over the Swat Valley in Pakistan in 2007. The Pakistani Government regained control of the region in 2009, but could never fully stabilize the area, which continues to suffer from violence. The Taliban—Islamic fundamentalists who had formed a government in Afghanistan between 1996 and 2001—are condemned internationally for their brutal treatment of women. Under their rule, women were forbidden an education, had to be accompanied by a male relative outside the home, and were required to wear a burqa (a garment that covers the head and body). Those who disobeyed were severely disciplined or beaten.

"She was attacked and shot by extremists who don't want girls to have an education and don't want girls to speak for themselves, and don't want girls to become leaders."

Former United States Secretary of State Hillary Clinton.

SHOULD OTHERS INTERFERE?

Do countries have the right to interfere in another country's cultural practices? While we should condemn extreme oppression, such as the Taliban's treatment of women, do Western countries have the right to restrict or ban their own citizens' traditional practices such as arranged marriages or women's head coverings?

Symbol of oppression?

Some people in Western countries such as the United States, France, Britain, and Canada believe that the Muslim tradition of women wearing head coverings is a symbol of their oppression. Although this may be true of some cases in which women or girls are forced to cover their heads, faces, or bodies, many Muslim women feel that head coverings are liberating and an honest reflection of their religious devotion. Are the views of some

HEAD COVERINGS

There are a wide variety of head coverings worn by women in the Muslim world. The hijab is a simple head scarf that covers the hair. In Saudi Arabia, women typically wear a niqab, which is a veil that covers the face, leaving the eyes visible. The chador is a full body cloak that is common in Iran and the khimar covers the shoulders, neck and hair, leaving the face exposed. Burqas are full head, face, and body coverings (shown left). In Turkey and France, burqas are banned in public.

Young Muslim girls start wearing the hijab from puberty, or sometimes earlier depending on the family traditions.

Mumsnet's "Let Girls Be Girls" campaign aims to ease the pressure on young Western girls to dress and wear make-up like young women.

people in these predominantly Christian but **secular** countries legitimate, or is it a form of **discrimination**?

Western women and the media

Is the treatment and depiction of women in the West any better than in Muslim cultures? Bombarded by images in the media, women are under pressure to look a certain way and are often **sexualized** from a very young age. Some argue that women who wear make-up and high heels are oppressed by harmful beauty standards. Violence against women still occurs in the West, with many women and girls becoming victims of sexual **harassment**, domestic abuse, rape, or psychological problems such as eating disorders.

DEBATE
Should the wearing of the burqa be banned?

YES
Extreme coverings such as burqas deprive women of identity and social interaction. It is a symbol of oppression and inequality between men and women, and can restrict a woman's vision and movement.

NO
We should respect Muslim traditions. Wearing the burqa helps women to follow their religious and personal beliefs. It is unfair to ban a burqa without being critical of how western media tells women to look.

GENDER VIOLENCE

In many parts of the world, sons are favored over daughters. This is because boys traditionally presented less of a financial burden on a family. Men were usually the main income earners, and women's families paid large dowries to future husbands. The lower status of girls also means that when resources are scarce, daughters might receive less food, medical care, and education than their brothers. In extreme cases, girl babies are so devalued that they are aborted before birth, abandoned after, or killed, so that a poor family can afford to keep their sons.

Missing girls

Gender discrimination, as shown in the view that girls are a burden on their families, can result in gender-based violence such as honor killings. It can also result in the abortion of female fetuses and the killing of infant girls, or female infanticide.

Female infanticide has led to serious gender imbalances in the populations of some Asian countries, including India, China, South Korea, and Singapore. UNICEF estimates that up to 50 million girls are missing from India's population. This is known as the "missing girls" phenomenon.

DOWRY

Across south Asia, forced marriages occur regularly and can sometimes be the most demeaning rite of passage a woman endures. For some marriages, the bride's family gives her to the highest bidder. For others, the bride's family pays a substantial dowry to the husband's family. Some men and their families, if unhappy with the dowry, resort to killing the bride. In India, the Ministry of Women and Child Development reported 8,455 known dowry murders in 2014.

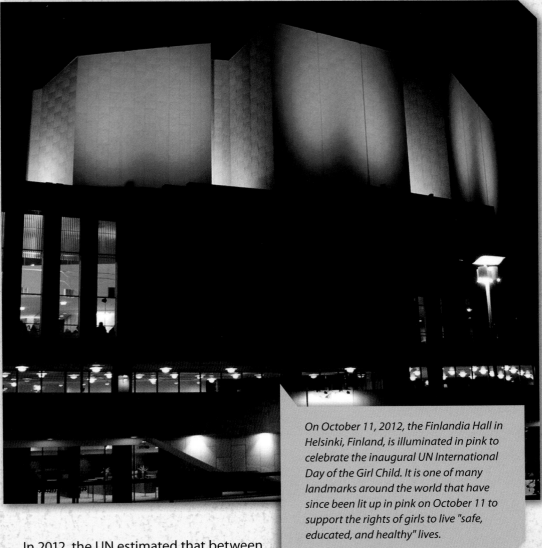

On October 11, 2012, the Finlandia Hall in Helsinki, Finland, is illuminated in pink to celebrate the inaugural UN International Day of the Girl Child. It is one of many landmarks around the world that have since been lit up in pink on October 11 to support the rights of girls to live "safe, educated, and healthy" lives.

In 2012, the UN estimated that between 33 million and 160 million girls had been aborted or were victims of infanticide. In China, the country's "one-child" policy tries to curb population increase by allowing families only one child. In parents' desire for their single child to be male, high numbers of female abortion and infanticide result if their firstborn is female.

"We want ourselves, and girls everywhere, to be seen as equals, in the eyes of others and in our own eyes."

Day of the Girl – U.S. organization

HOW DOES THE MEDIA ACT?

The ways the media depicts issues of violence against women are important influences on how we view the issues. In some cases, it can help expose the plight of victims and generate change. In other cases, the media contributes to the problem by promoting biases or stereotypes about women.

A force for good

Social media is relatively new, much of it having been around only since the early to mid 2000s. It can help to raise awareness and inspire people to engage in social activism. For example, when more than 200 Nigerian schoolgirls were kidnapped in April 2014 by the Islamist terrorist group Boko Haram, people took to social media to spread the word. The hashtag #BringBackOurGirls was tweeted more than 2 million times. Stories such as this show the power the media has to influence society in a positive way, by bringing important issues to our attention and generating debate and change. For

Women at a rally publicize the #BringBackOurGirls effort. The rally was held on Capital Hill in Washington, D.C. Although many influential people including U.S. First Lady Michelle Obama tweeted the #BringBackOurGirls message, most of the girls and young women are still missing. This has led some people to question whether social media activism can be successful.

this reason, the media is used as an important tool by governments and even organizations working for women. The Half The Sky Movement, for example, is a multimedia project that tackles the oppression of women globally through books, television programs, Internet sites, Facebook, video games, and other digital forms.

A destructive power

While the media can be a force for good, it can also contribute to and justify violence against women. Images of submissive, **objectified**, and **victimized** women are often seen in advertisements, on TV, in movies, and on the Internet. **Pornography**—which makes up 12 percent of all websites—commonly presents even more extreme examples of violence, such as female subordination and rape. On these websites, violence against women is made acceptable, if not the norm.

We should also be aware of how news reports present violence against women. Stories might **sensationalize** large-scale violence, downplaying more common examples of domestic abuse or rape. Some networks might imply violence against women only happens in certain parts of the world, even though it is a global issue.

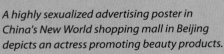
A highly sexualized advertising poster in China's New World shopping mall in Beijing depicts an actress promoting beauty products.

"I'd like you to imagine a world where women are valued for what they say and what they do, rather than the way they look."

Caroline Heldman, TED Talks, February 2014

WEAPONS OF WAR

Violence against women, in the forms of rape, mutilation, and forced sexual slavery, has been used as a tactic of war throughout history. It can occur on small and large scales, and is even sometimes actively encouraged by military leaders who use it as a deliberate strategy to degrade women in areas of conflict.

Psychological warfare

Psychological warfare is a tactic used in war to reduce an enemy's confidence or influence their thinking. Violence against women is used in warfare to humiliate an enemy and shatter communities. It was also sometimes used as ethnic cleansing, in which women would be impregnated by opposing soldiers so that their babies would not carry on the ethnicity of the men in their country. The systematic rape of women in **Bosnia** in the 1990s and the estimated 200,000 women raped during the battle for Bangladeshi independence in 1971 are two examples of this horrific tactic.

Three survivors of rape during the 1971 war for independence attend a ceremony in Dhaka, the capital of Bangladesh. The use of rape as a war tactic in Bangladesh meant that many survivors, because of their family or community's religious and cultural beliefs, were shamed for the abuse they suffered.

These Congolese soldiers are attending a seven-month training program in field sanitation, gender-based violence, and military professionalism in the Democratic Republic of the Congo (DR Congo) in 2010 as part of an operation led by the United States Africa Command.

War crime

For a long time, it was simply accepted that violence against women was inevitable during times of conflict. Because of this view, few efforts were made to prosecute perpetrators. In 1998, the UN passed a resolution classifying sexual violence in conflict, including rape, as a war crime. On September 24, 2013, 113 countries endorsed a UN Declaration of Commitment to End Sexual Violence in Conflict. The UN wanted to raise awareness of the crimes, and respond to and reduce sexual violence in conflict zones.

> **"In Bosnia, systematic rape was used as part of the strategy of ethnic cleansing. Women were raped so they could give birth to a Serbian baby."**
>
> **Doctors Without Borders/Médicins Sans Frontiéres, humanitarian organization**

CONFLICT ZONES

- In the Democratic Republic of the Congo, approximately 1,100 rapes are being reported each month, with an average of 36 women and girls raped every day. It is believed that more than 200,000 women have suffered from sexual violence there since armed conflict began in 1996.
- The rape and sexual violation of women and girls is pervasive in the conflict in the Darfur region of Sudan, which began in 2003.
- Between 250,000 and 500,000 women were raped during the 1994 genocide in Rwanda.

MASS RAPE OF CONGOLESE WOMEN

Two of the most deadly wars in Africa began in 1996 in the DR Congo. Since the outbreak of wars in 1996 and 1998, 5 million people have lost their lives and at least 200,000 women have been raped by the Congolese army, the armies of neighboring countries, **militias**, gangs, and other civilians.

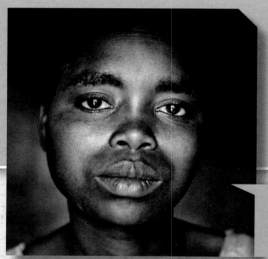

NEWS FLASH

Date: Since 1998
Location: Democratic Republic of the Congo, Central Africa
Perpetrators: Congolese Army, local militias, and gangs
Victim: Estimated 200,000 women and girls (men and boys also raped)
Types of violence: Rape and torture

This woman is one of the thousands of survivors who have been used as so-called "weapons of war" in the DR Congo.

A dangerous place

Although the Congolese war officially ended in 2003, fighting has carried on in the east of the country and with it, sexual violence continues. Some reports, in more recent years, claim that the number of rapes is far higher than 200,000. According to the *American Journal of Public Health*, there were 400,000 rapes in one year, spanning from 2006 to 2007, alone.

The types of violence inflicted on civilians, young and old, include rape, forced prostitution and sexual slavery, torture, genital mutilation, and murder. Reports tell of soldiers entering villages

Hundreds of Congolese women, victims of sexual violence, have taken refuge in the village of Buganga—known as the village of victims. Mama Masika (in the center), once a victim herself, helps them start a new life there.

and towns and conducting brutal mass rapes, many having been ordered to rape by their superior officers. The rape of men and boys is also common. Many of the rape victims are adolescent girls, with some reports claiming that 10 percent of victims are children under the age of 10.

Some efforts have been made to prevent the **atrocities**. The UN pressured Congolese army generals to prosecute soldiers accused of sexual violence, and several military leaders have been charged with sexual violence by the International Criminal Court. In November 2013, after months of international pressure, 39 soldiers were put on trial in the eastern Congo. In general, however, human rights organizations point out that the Congolese government has done little to prosecute the perpetrators or provide adequate help for the rape victims.

"I was just coming back from the river to fetch water...Two soldiers came up to me and told me that if I refuse to sleep with them, they will kill me. They beat me and ripped my clothes. One of the soldiers raped me..."

15-year-old girl, Minova, South Kivu, DR Congo, Human Rights Watch

THE EFFECTS OF RAPE

What effect does rape during times of conflict have on women and their communities? How does all sexual violence affect victims and survivors and how does it impact a country's status and economy? Could it be considered a worldwide epidemic?

During conflict

The effects of rape and sexual violence during conflict are far-reaching. Medical repercussions can include broken limbs, pregnancy, transmission of **sexually transmitted infections** (STIs), severe internal injury, infertility, and death. Psychologically, victims can suffer from post-traumatic stress, **depression**, and other mental illness. Many, in an effort to cope with their abuse, engage in harmful behaviors such as drug and alcohol abuse or unsafe sex. Some have attempted or committed suicide. Rape victims can also be isolated by their families and communities, abandoned by intimate partners and, in extreme cases, murdered in the belief that they have brought shame to their family and community.

Global consequences

Victims of sexual violence suffer from a huge range of physical and psychological problems, which often restrict their ability to participate fully in the world around them. They also often experience serious

WHAT ARE THE NUMBERS?

- Victims of non-partner attacks are 2.6 times more likely to experience mental health issues compared with women who have not experienced violence.
- Those abused by their partners are almost twice as likely to have mental health issues compared with women who were victims of non-partner attacks.

This Allied army officer in Rangoon, Myanmar (Burma) in August 1945 is talking to a young Chinese woman who had been abused in one of the Japanese army's "comfort battalions"–official military brothels, or places where soldiers would visit women who had been forced into prostitution.

and bringing perpetrators to justice, as well as the indirect costs of lost employment when survivors are unable to work. A 2009 report in the United Kingdom estimated the yearly cost of domestic violence alone to be around $23.2 billion.

ongoing health problems. A 2014 World Health Organization report indicated that around a third of all women worldwide experience some form of sexual violence. In many countries, the figure is significantly higher.

Financial cost?

Is there a global financial cost to sexual violence? The human pain and suffering inflicted on victims of sexual violence is almost impossible to describe using numbers. However, there are costs involved in treating the health of survivors

The International Rescue Committee (IRC) provides psychosocial workers to help rape survivors in South Kivu, DR Congo, access the services they need to begin their recovery.

"Worldwide, it has been estimated that violence against women is as serious a cause of death and incapacity among women of reproductive age as cancer, and a greater cause of ill-health than traffic accidents and malaria combined."

World Health Organization

CHALLENGING VIOLENCE

How are people around the world challenging violence against women? What can we all do to bring about the changes that are needed to free women from the fear of violent abuse and the consequences of such attacks?

Men and boys

Everyone should speak out against violence against women, and men and boys have a crucial role to play. They can teach others to embrace equality between the sexes, raise awareness about the consequences of violence against women, support the victims and survivors of violence, and be positive role models.

A wave of protest

Angered by the extreme violence against women, many women have engaged in protests. During Egypt's political uprisings

Men are vital allies in the struggle to end gender violence. This man is taking part in an International Women's Day rally in New York. International Women's Day is held March 8 every year and promotes gender equality.

The HeForShe campaign, promoted here by actress and UN Goodwill Ambassador Emma Watson and UN Secretary General Ban Ki-moon, promotes gender equality as an issue for all genders and not just women.

between 2011 and 2013, mob-led attacks on women and the subsequent beating of female protestors by the Egyptian military led thousands of women to march in protest through the streets of Cairo. There are also changes happening on more formal levels. Emma Watson made waves in September 2014 when she spoke at the launch of the UN's HeForShe campaign, which invites all people to take part in a global movement for gender equality. The movement has the support of governments and organizations.

ONE BILLION RISING

The One Billion Rising campaign, launched by American playwright Eve Ensler in 2013, held rallies in more than 190 countries across the world on February 12 (see page 5). Protests ranged from the first ever flash mob in Mogadishu in Somalia to 13,000 women forming human chains in Bangladesh's cities. "One billion" refers to the statistic that one in three women will be raped or beaten in their lifetime, or about one billion women worldwide.

"Men must teach each other that real men do not violate or oppress women – and that a woman's place is not just in the home or the field, but in schools and offices and boardrooms."

UN Secretary-General Ban Ki-moon

GANG RAPE IN DELHI

On December 16, 2012, 23-year-old student Jyoti Singh Pandey and a male friend boarded an off-duty charter bus in South Delhi, India. On the bus were six men who proceeded to beat the male unconscious, then drag the woman to the back of the bus where she was beaten and raped while the bus drove around Delhi.

NEWS FLASH

Date: December 16, 2012
Location: Munirka, Delhi, India
Perpetrators: Six men, including a 17-year-old juvenile
Victim: 23-year-old Jyoti Singh Pandey
Types of violence: Beatings and gang rape, with extreme brutality

To comply with Indian law, the victim's name was not released to the media. Her father (left) later released her name as Jyoti Singh Pandey in the hope that it would help other victims come forward.

The assault

Jyoti suffered horrific injuries as a result of her assault. After several attempts by surgeons to save her life, she died on December 29. The following year, all six attackers were arrested and tried, with four of the perpetrators sentenced to death by hanging on September 13. One of the men died in custody before the trial and the other attacker, a 17-year-old, was given the maximum sentence for a juvenile—three years.

Outpouring of anger

The incident unleashed an **unprecedented** outpouring of anger and grief in India. Citizens were angry at the authorities' inability to prevent the attack and quickly prosecute the attackers. Within days of the attack, thousands of people protested in India, with further protests in the countries of Bangladesh, Nepal, Sri Lanka, and Pakistan. All of the protests called for an end to sexual violence, legal reform, and a change in harmful attitudes toward women.

Men and women in New Delhi, India, gathered on March 5, 2013 to protest against the rising number of rape incidents in the city.

The media gave the incident a lot of global news coverage, so that Pandey's story could not be ignored. This led organizations, including the UN, to demand that the Indian government bring about radical reforms to make women's lives safer. The Indian government has responded with amendments to the law, the introduction of fast-track courts, and improvements in police procedure. As a result, more women in India have the resources and support to report their rapes—but many still struggle to find justice.

EVE TEASING

In India, sexual harassment on public transport is common. The media often calls it the slang term "eve teasing." Indian activists have repeatedly argued that slang terms like these contribute to the widespread acceptance of sexual harassment in public places.

WHO WAS TO BLAME?

Lawyers defending the rapists in Delhi pointed some of the blame at the victim, claiming she should not have been out at night, and that they had never heard of a "respected lady" being raped in India. Why is victim-blaming so common when it comes to sexual assault and violence against women?

Indian women in Parmandapur, a rural area of Uttar Pradesh, participate in an awareness course on sexual violence.

Rape culture

Media coverage of the rape in Delhi highlighted the plight of women in India who suffer from harassment and discrimination throughout their lives. This gender inequality, some say, fuels a "**rape culture**" in India. The widespread coverage of Pandey's assault prompted open debate about the issue of violence against women. Social media also played an important part in mobilizing support for women's rights, with people voicing their anger through Twitter, Facebook, and other social media platforms.

> **"Sexual violence is no stranger to Indian society. What is new, is the way in which cases, like those I've mentioned, are being picked up by the press and talked about around the family dining table. Before the turmoil of the Delhi rape, the weight of sharam or shame that surrounded the sexual violation of women prevented most from reporting attacks even to their families."**

Anita Anand, *The Telegraph*, September 11, 2013.

In the West

Some critics have suggested that the media's coverage in the West demonized Indian society, saying that its treatment of women was barbaric, while ignoring the enormity of Western rape culture. *The Wall Street Journal* reported that in India, just over a quarter of alleged rapes result in a conviction. However, in the United States, only 24 percent of alleged rapes result in an initial arrest. Similarly, the British Broadcasting Corporation (BBC) stated that a woman is raped in Delhi every 14 hours, equating to 625 victims per year. In England and Wales, with a population about 3.5 times the size of Delhi, the number of recorded rapes of women is far higher—9,509 per year.

INTERNATIONAL WOMEN'S DAY

MILLION WOMEN RISE

MILLIONWOMENRISE.COM

Women gather in London, England, in March 2014 to support Million Women Rise, an annual event held to raise awareness about violence against women.

COMBATING RAPE CULTURE

On February 28, 2016, Lady Gaga's performance of "Til it Happens to You" at the Oscars made waves in the news and on social media. The award-nominated song drew attention to the prevalence of rape culture in the United States and throughout the world, and pushed listeners to take a hard look at the ways sexual violence against women can be ignored in society.

One in Five

Lady Gaga's song was written for the documentary *The Hunting Ground*, in which college girls across the United States speak out about their rapes on their college campuses and the covering-up of their abuse by varying officials. The girls explain that their cases had not been investigated thoroughly, nor had the perpetrators been held accountable for their actions. This is because legal systems often make it difficult for victims to prove that they were raped, with perpetrators claiming that the sex was consensual, or something women agreed to. The documentary shows how damaging and wrong this is.

Survivors of sexual assault joined Lady Gaga on stage during her performance. According to the documentary, one in five women on college campuses is sexually assaulted.

Activists are starting to make real change in the way sexual assaults are treated on college campuses. States and individual schools are adopting laws that make hearing verbal consent mandatory for any sexual contact. Here, New York Governor Andrew Cuomo signs the New York "Enough Is Enough" law.

Victim shaming

Rape culture means that sexual violence has been made "normal" in society through widespread beliefs and attitudes about women and men. Often, this has to do with old, patriarchal values that objectify women as objects of a man's pleasure.

Often, rape culture involves victim shaming, in which the blame for the sexual violence is placed on the victim. Some common arguments to this effect might be that the victim is to blame for consuming alcohol or drugs, wearing revealing clothing, or being friendly with her attacker. Too often, victim shaming stops a woman from coming forward after she has been assaulted.

"I need the world to start believing survivors. But even more, I need the kindhearted part of the world to recognize that sexual violence is not a solved problem."

Jacqueline Lin, survivor, Stanford University

TAKING ACTION TO END VIOLENCE

So what can we do to end violence against women?
How can we change attitudes where women are treated as
inferior, and where violence is protected by cultural practices,
hidden behind closed doors, and deemed acceptable?

Learn about violence

Taking time to learn about violence against women, in all its various forms, is an important first step. It will help you to recognize violence if it happens to you or to someone you know, or when you read about victims of abuse and violence in the news or on other types of media.

Positions of power

Passing laws that criminalize violence against women is another important way to change unacceptable behavior toward women. It can help to prevent violence, protect victims, and punish attackers. However, passing laws is not always enough. Laws have to be enforced. More importantly, cultural attitudes towards women have to change. This process takes much longer, and must involve every level of society. People in government and positions of power can help to change

By not ignoring injustices, or not leaving the fight to older generations, young women are proving they are key players in ending gender-based violence.

44

Women of all ages march in a rally demanding an end to violence against women in Lahore, Pakistan. Women who work for gender equality often risk their own safety and lives because some men do not want to give up power and become enraged when they feel their position is threatened.

laws from the top down, but people from all walks of life need to recognize violence, voice their opposition to it, and demand change. Communities must bring violence against women and girls, hidden or protected by tradition or cultural practice, out from behind closed doors and collectively refuse to accept it as normal behavior. Above all, gender equality needs to be seen as a goal that benefits all of society, and not just women.

What can you do?

Learn about the types of violence that happen in your own community and across the world. Talk about it at home, at school, and with your friends and family. Join global campaigns such as One Billion Rising, recognize and speak against **sexism** in the media, and consider all perspectives when reading about violence against women in the news.

"Violence against women is always a violation of human rights; it is always a crime; and it is always unacceptable. Let us take this issue with the deadly seriousness that it deserves."

UN Secretary-General Ban Ki-moon

GLOSSARY

abortion
An operation or other medical procedure to terminate a pregnancy

atrocities
Acts of extreme violence or cruelty

Bosnia
A region of of Bosnia and Herzegovina, a country in southereastern Europe

caste
A social group limited to those of the same social standing or class, usually associated with hereditary classes into which the population in India is historically divided

consequence
Something that happens as a result of actions that have already occurred

criminalize
To make something illegal

depression
A mental illness characterized by intense sadness that affects a person's thoughts, feelings, actions, and attitude toward others

discrimination
Unfair or unusual treatment of someone because of their race, age, or sex

domestic violence
Violence that occurs within the home, usually by a partner or spouse

dowries
Property or money that is given by parents to a daughter when she marries, which then belongs to her new family

economic
Relating to the financial situation of a family or community

ethnic cleansing
The killing, or expulsion, of all members of a certain ethnic group

ethnicity
Belonging to a certain group with a common racial, national, social, cultural, or religious background

female genital mutilation (FGM)
Procedures, sometimes rooted in ethnic or cultural traditions, that remove some or all of the external part of a woman's vagina

genocide
The murder of a large number of people, especially those of a particular race, nationality, or social group

grooming
The tactic used by pedophiles or other sexual predators to gain the trust of their victims

harassment
Aggressive pestering that intimidates victims, putting them under pressure

HIV
Human Immunodeficiency Virus—the virus that causes AIDS

Indigenous
Referring to people who have lived in, or are native to, a region for a long time

infanticide
The murder of an infant, particularly a baby who is less than one year old

migrant

A person who moves from one place to another, especially when looking for work

militia

Fighting forces made up of citizen volunteers or non-professional soldiers

objectified

Treated someone in a degrading way, as though they were an object rather than a human being

oppressive

Describing prolonged cruel, harsh, or unfair treatment that causes victims distress

patriarchal

Describing a society, culture, or belief that men should hold power and control

perpetrator

A person who deliberately does something harmful or illegal

pornography

Writing or images that describe or show sex acts

prostitution

Participating in sex acts for payment

psychological

Describing anything affecting the mind and a person's emotional condition

rape

Forcing another person to have sex against his or her will

rape culture

Describing a society or community in which rape is made to be a "normal" occurrence, in that the victim is often blamed for their assault and perpetrators are rarely convicted

secular

Relating to the separation of religion from law or government

sensationalize

In the media, to present a news story in a way that exaggerates or misinforms consumers to gain as much interest as possible

sexism

The stereotyping or discrimination against a person based on their sex

sexualized

Associated a person or object with sex or ascribed sexual characteristics to them

sexually transmitted infection

Also known as STIs, this covers a range of diseases passed from one person to another when participating in sex acts

systematically

Describing something done within or through a system, or through an orderly procedure or method

unprecedented

Has never happened before

victimized

Treating someone unfairly or unjustly; singled out a person or group for abuse

war crimes

Crimes that are against the accepted rules of war, including genocide and the use of banned weapons

Western world

Referring to the part of the world made up of Western countries, such as the United States; is also used to refer to the culture shared by people in those countries

INDEX

A

abortion 4, 26, 27
Afghanistan 23
alcohol 9, 10, 34, 43
Amnesty International 16
Asian countries 19, 21, 26

B

Ban Ki-moon 37, 45
Bangladesh 30, 37, 39
Bosnia 6, 30, 31
Burma 35
burqa 23, 24, 25

C

Cairo 37
Canada 17, 36
CEOP 13
chador 24
China 26, 27, 29
Ciudad Juárez 16, 17
Clinton, Hillary 23
Congo, DR 15, 31, 32, 33, 35

D

Darfur 31
Davies, Peter 13
Day of the Girl Child 27
Delhi 38, 39, 40, 41
Derby 10, 11, 12
domestic workers 19
dowry 26
drugs 10, 17, 17, 34, 43
"Dru's Law" 11

E

Egypt 36, 37
Emma Watson 37
"Enough Is Enough" law 43
Ethiopia 9

exploitation 13, 16, 18

F

Facebook 29, 40
FGM 4, 20
forced marriage 4, 26
France 24

G

Germany 13
grooming 10, 11, 12, 13

H

Hague, William 6, 45
hijab 24, 25
HIV 6
Hong Kong 29
honor violence 21
human trafficking 4, 25, 16, 18, 19

I

India 9, 18, 26, 38, 39, 40, 41, 44
infanticide 26, 27
Internet 9, 13, 29
intimate partner violence 4, 7, 9, 14

J

Japan 6, 9, 35
Jolie, Angelina 6

K

khimar 24
Kosovo 19

L

Lady Gaga 42
London 6, 41, 45

M

Médicins Sans Frontières 31
Mexico 16, 17
Million Women Rise 41
Minova, DR Congo 33
Moldova 19
Muslims 24, 25
Myanmar 35

N

Native women, Canada 17
New Delhi 39
New York 5, 36, 43
Nigeria 28
niqab 24

O

Obaid-Chinoy, Sharmeen 21
Obama, Michelle 28
One Billion Rising 5, 37, 45
one-child policy 27

P

Pakistan 12, 13, 21, 22, 23, 39, 45
Pandey, Jyoti Singh 38, 39, 40
pornography 29
prostitution 4, 15, 17, 19, 32
psychological warfare 30

R

Rangoon 35
rape 4, 6, 7, 10, 15, 16, 21, 25, 29, 30, 31, 32, 33, 34, 35, 37, 38, 39, 40, 41, 42, 43, 45
rape culture 40, 41, 42, 43
Russia 7
Rwanda 6, 31

S

Simpson, O.J. 14
Singapore 26
Soroptimist International 19
South Kivu 33, 35
South Korea 26
Sri Lanka 39
sterility 21
Sudan 31

T

Taliban 22, 23, 24
The Hunting Ground 42
Toronto 17, 36
Turkey 24
Twitter 28, 40

U

United Kingdom (UK) 10, 12, 13, 23, 35
UNICEF 15, 26
United Nations (UN) 4, 5, 6, 9, 18, 23, 27, 31, 37, 45
United States 11, 13, 14, 15, 31, 41, 42, 43

V

veil 24

W

Women's Day 36
World Health Organization (WHO) 8, 9, 35
World War II 6

Y

Yousafzai, Malala 22, 23